OCEAN ODDITIES

AN ADULT COLORING BOOK

Facebook: Facebook.com/dianananaferrer

Instagram: @artbynana305

Twitter: @artbynana305

Copyright © 2017 Diana NaNa Ferrer

Diana NaNa Ferrer

Use this page to test your art materials.

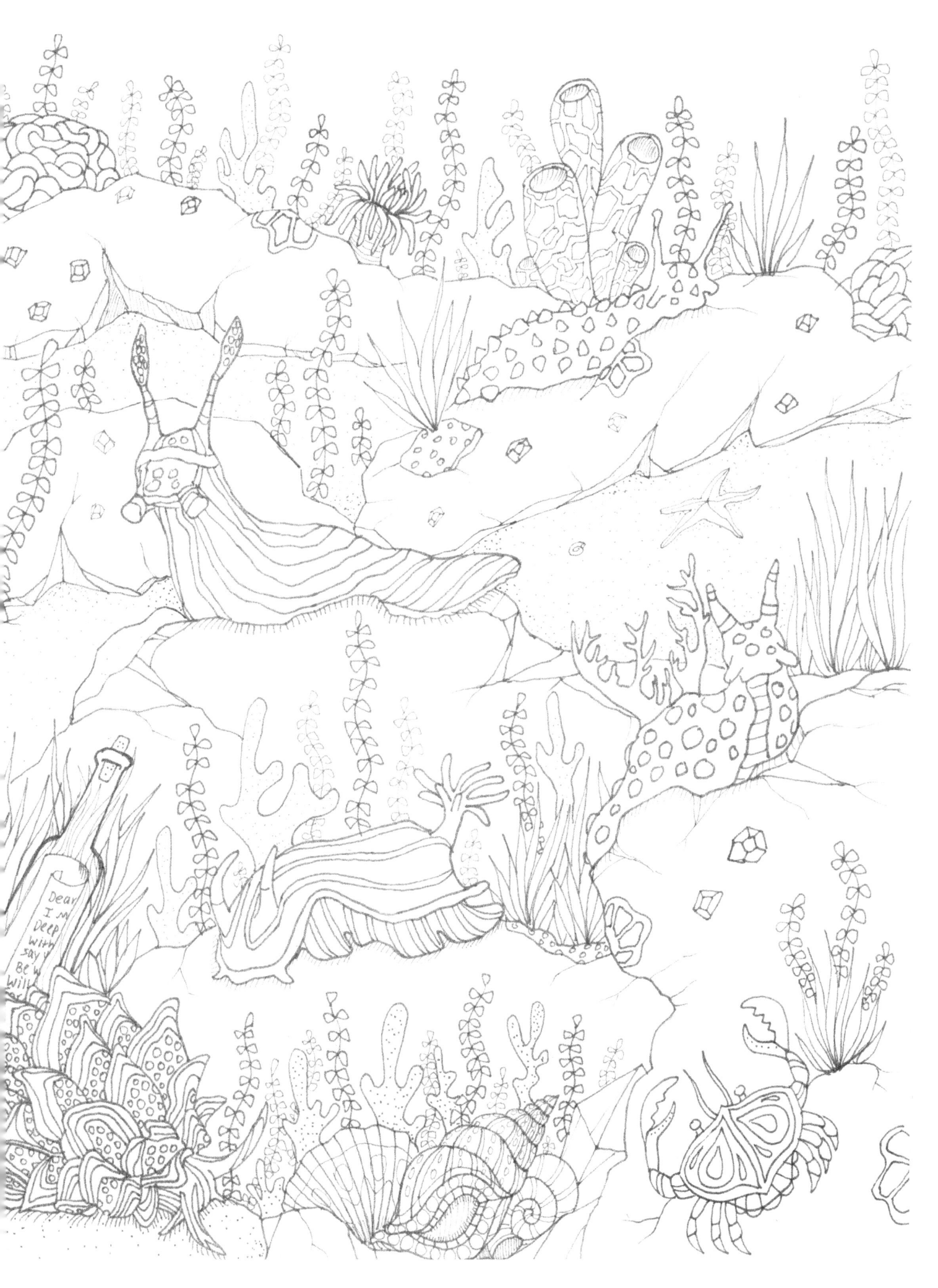

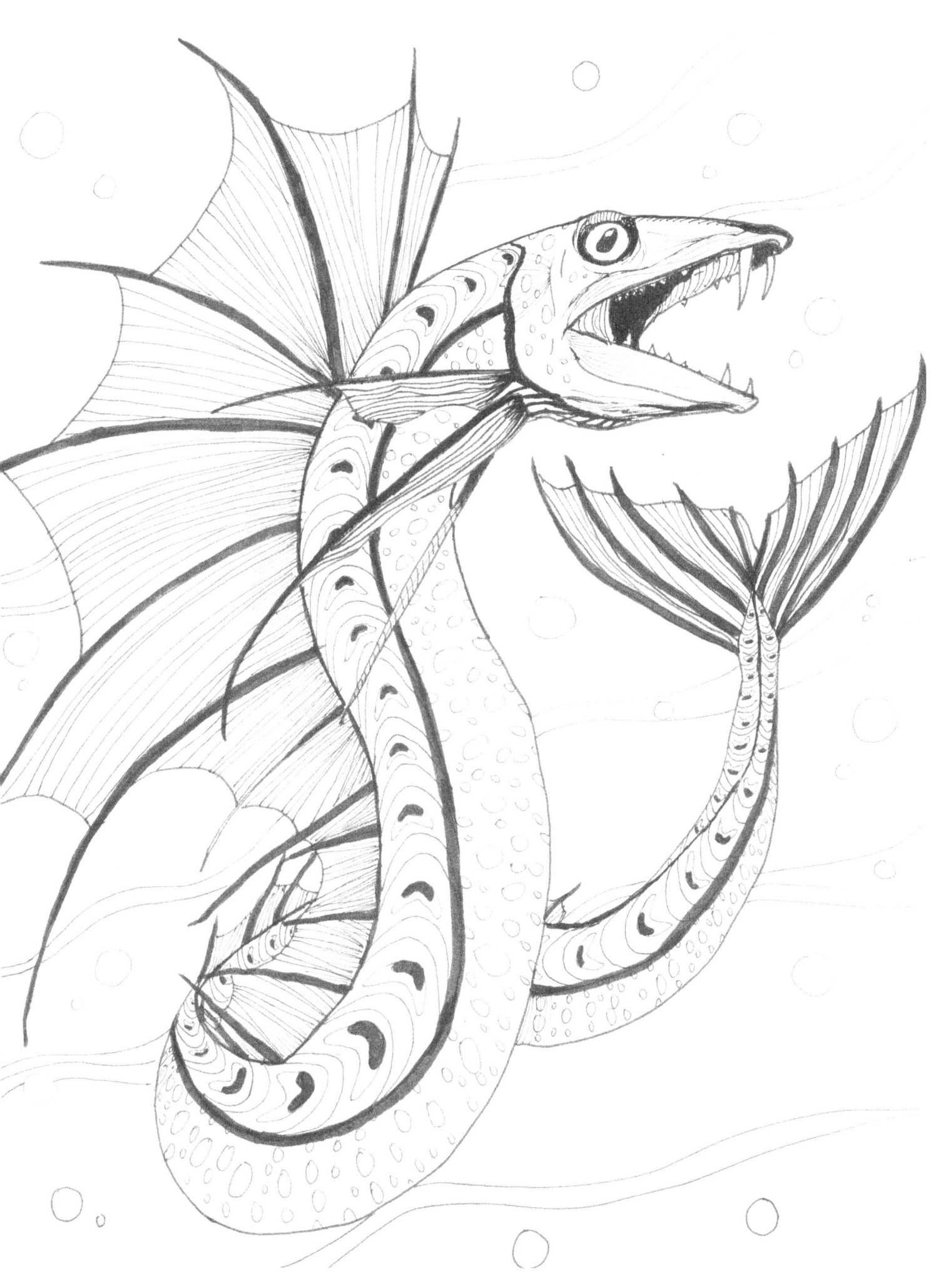

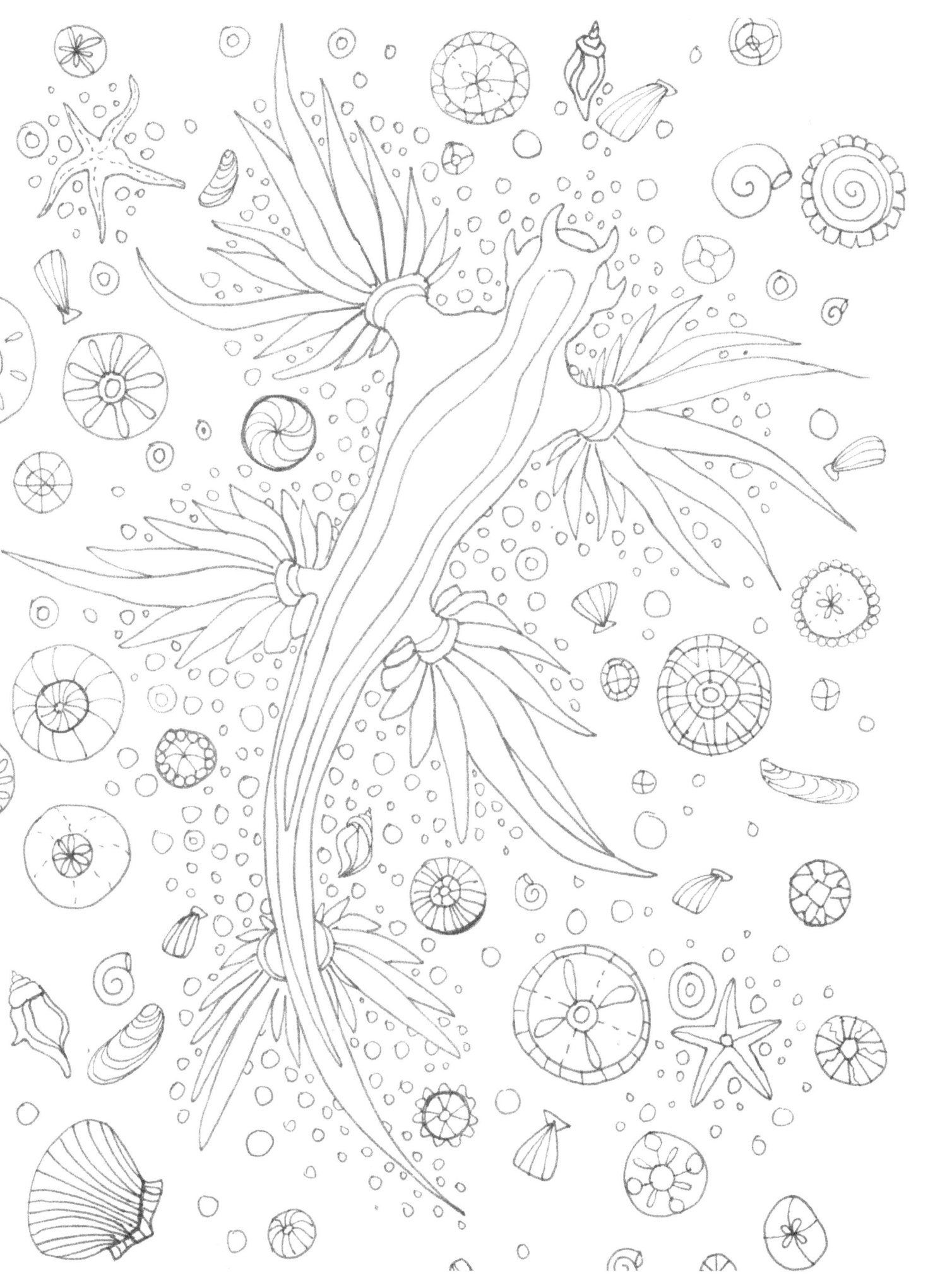

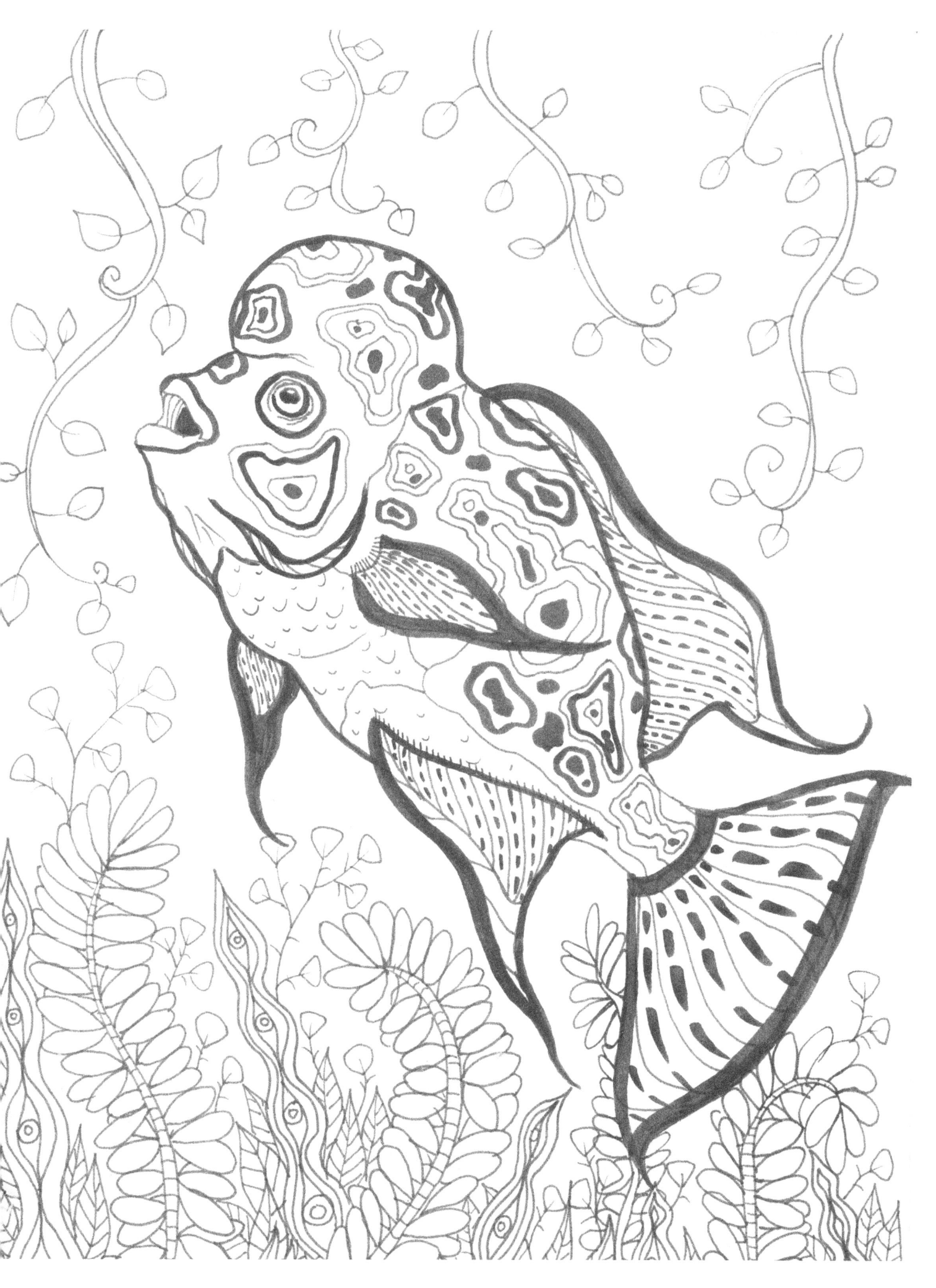

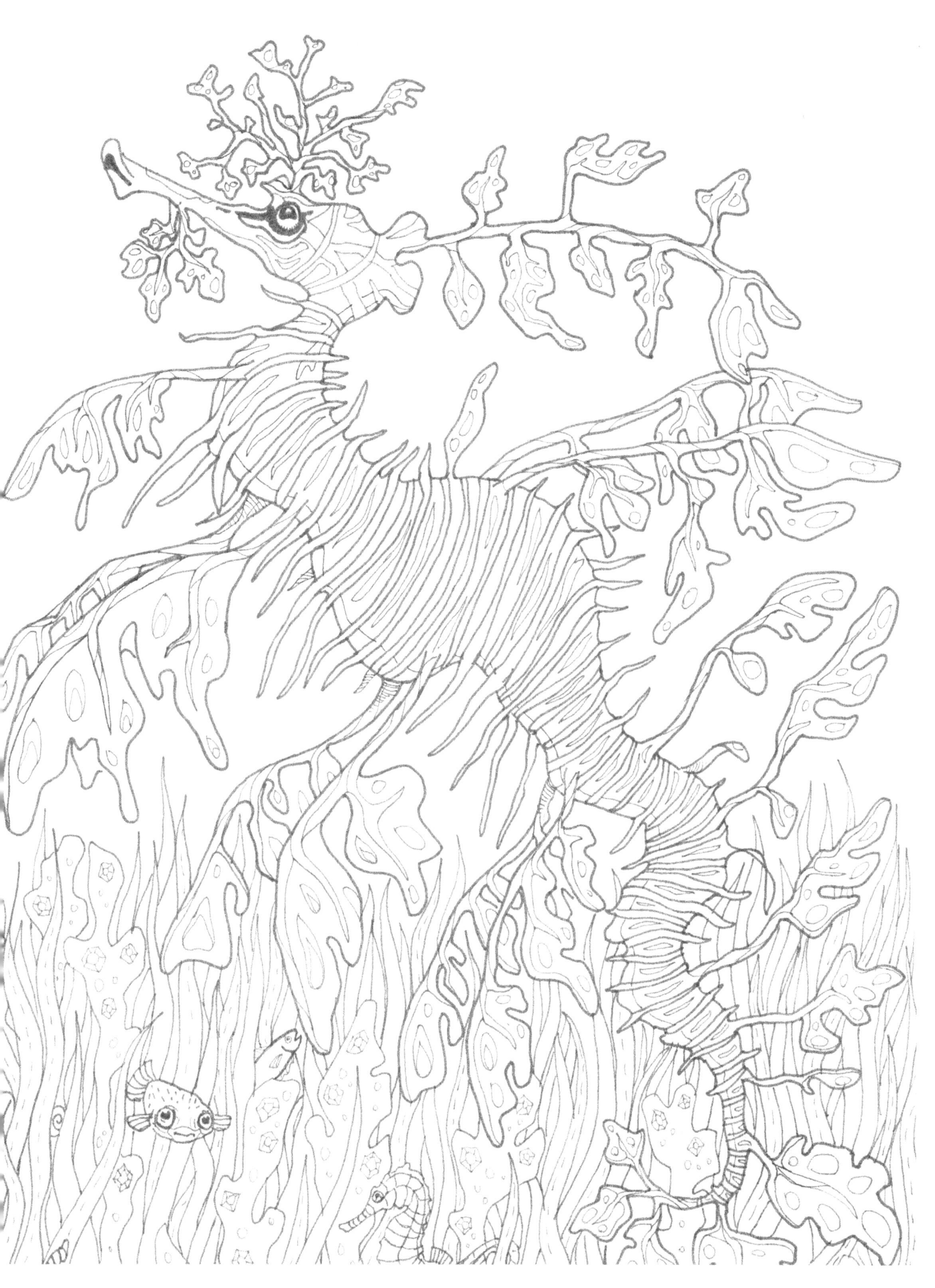

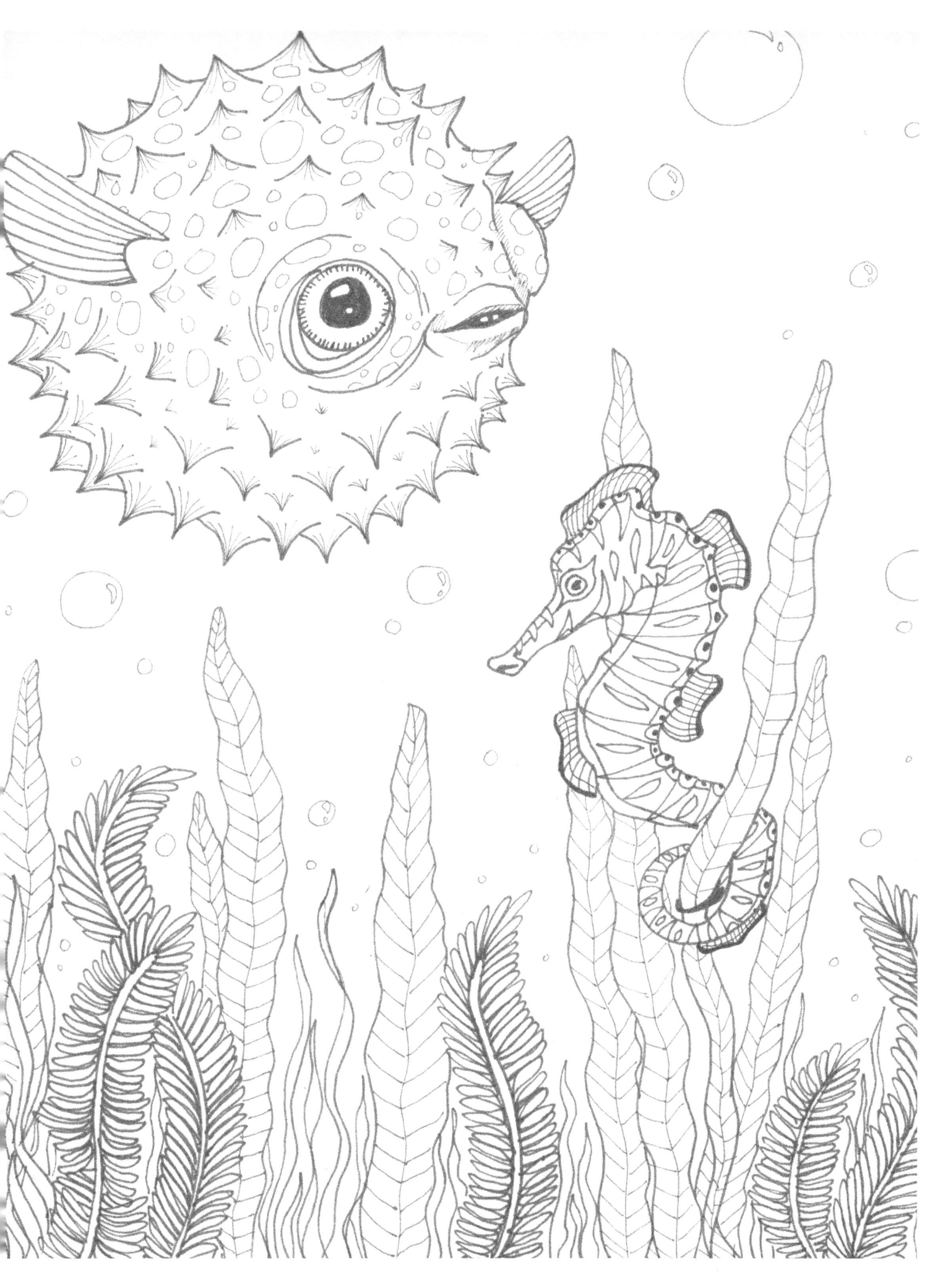

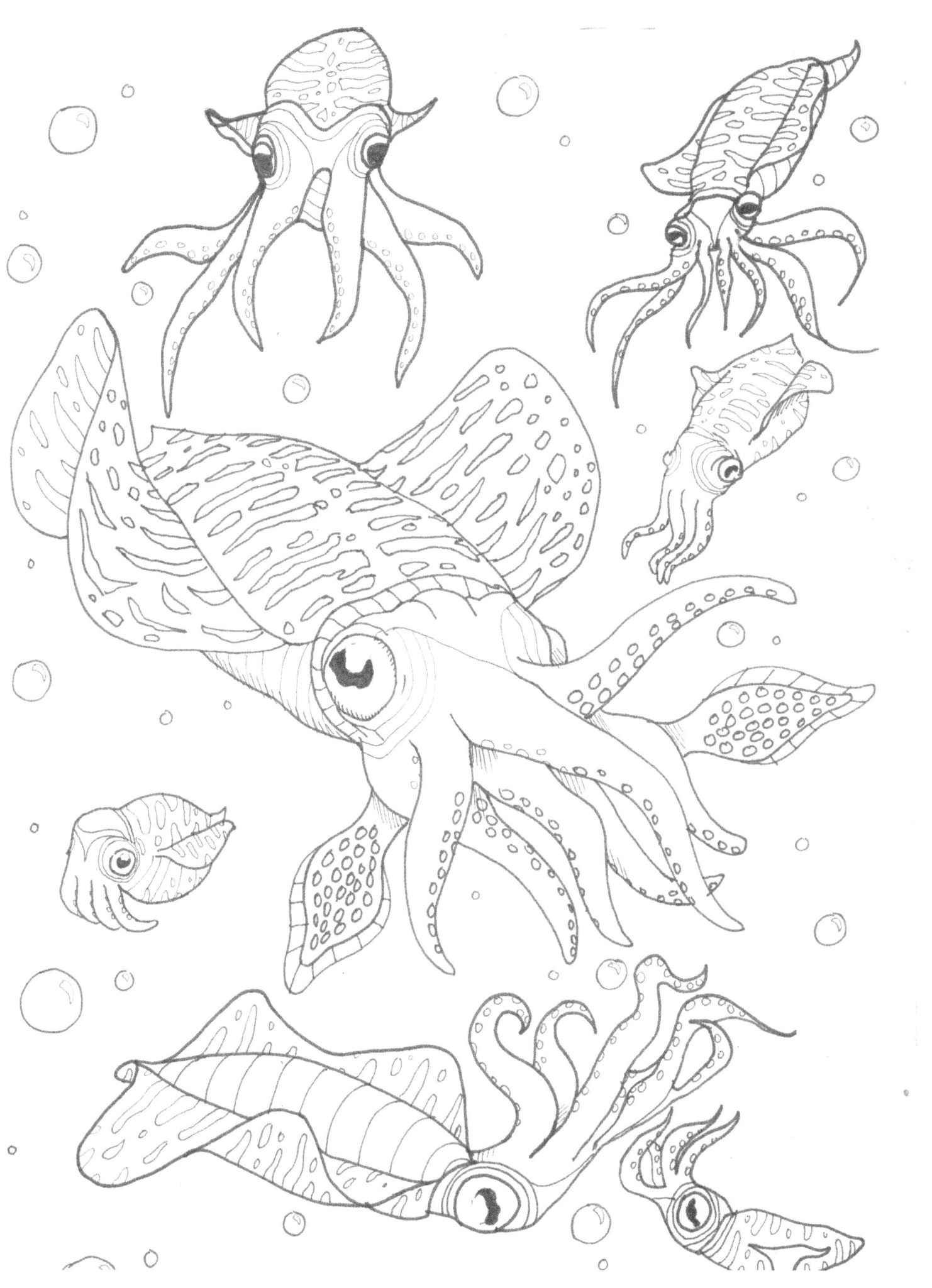

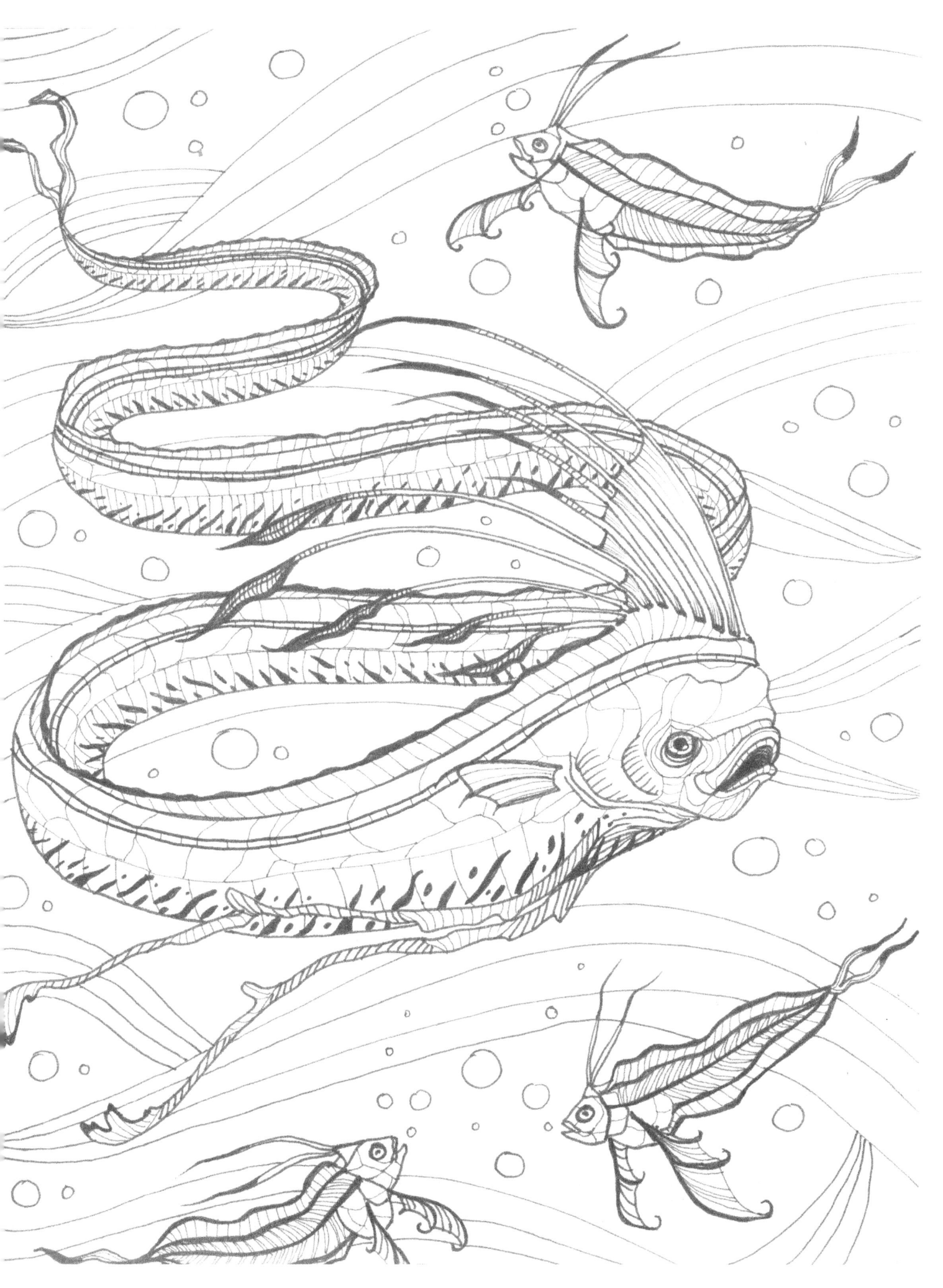

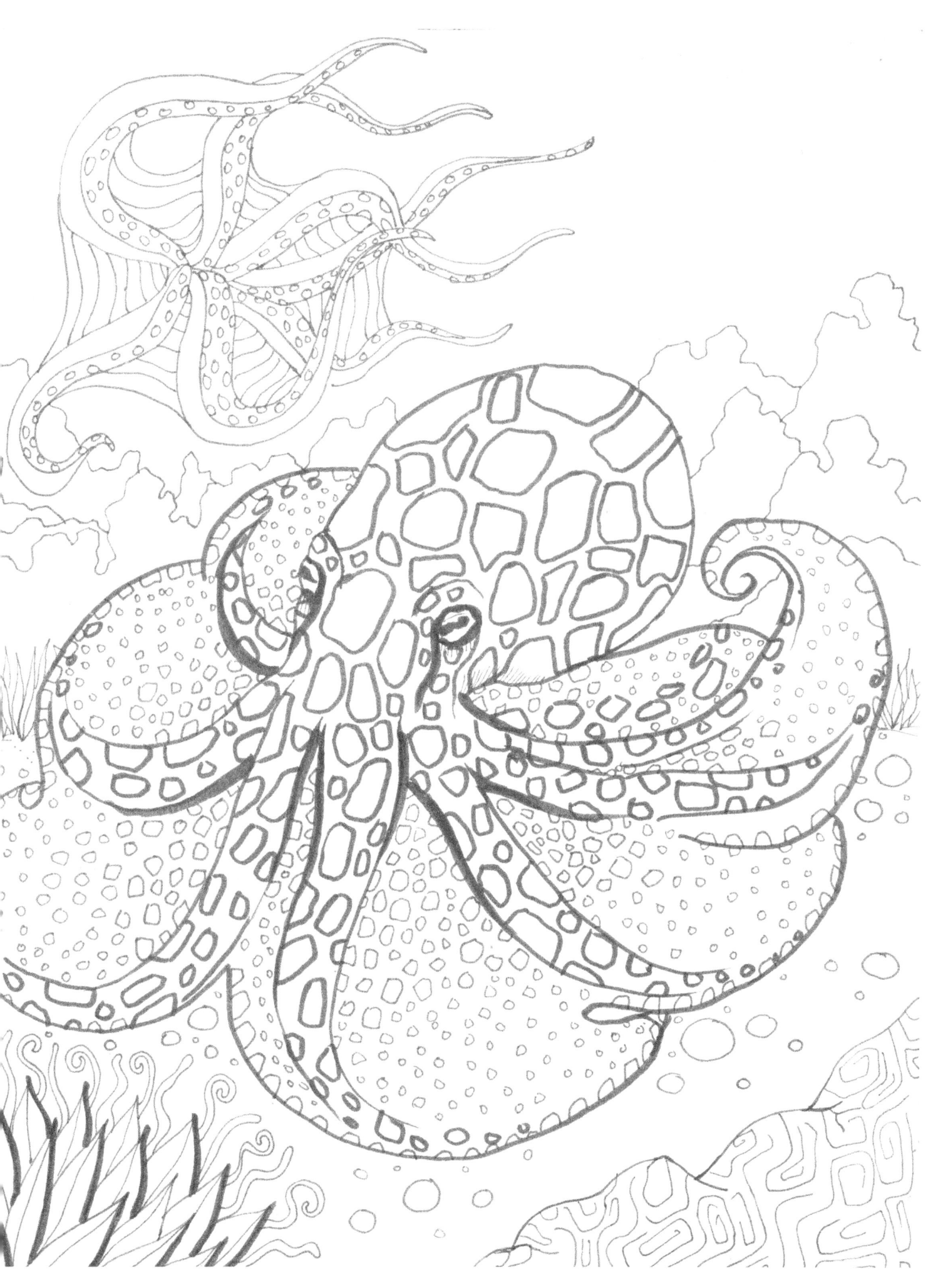

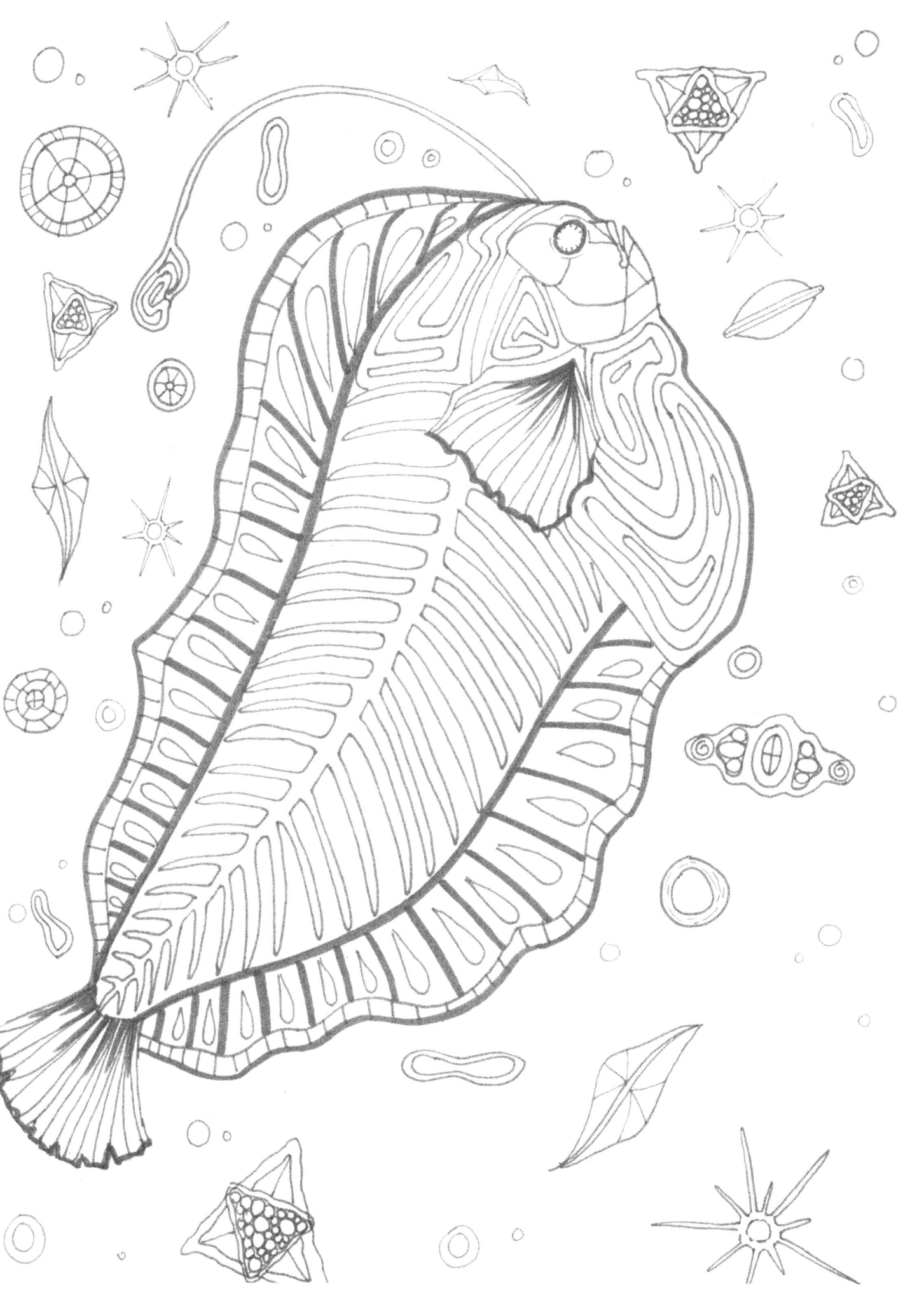

www.ingramcontent.com/pod-product-compliance
Lightning Source LLC
Chambersburg PA
CBHW081320180526
45170CB00007B/2794